Special Education at Home:

Out-of-the-Box Learning for Out-of-the-Box Learners

By: Shawna Wingert

Not The Former Things

Table of Contents

Part One: "Special" Education

Chapter 1 – Our Story

Chapter 2 – Why Special Education?

Part Two: The Reality

Chapter 3 – Am I Qualified to Homeschool My Child with Special Needs?

Chapter 4 – Getting Started

Chapter 5 – Expectations vs. Reality

Chapter 6 – Sleep Matters

Chapter 7 – Life Skills

Part Three: The Learning

Chapter 8 - Feeling the Pressure to Recreate School

Chapter 9 – Embracing the Actual vs. the Idea of How It Would Be

Chapter 10 – Learning Everywhere BUT Home

Chapter 11 – Teaching My Dyslexic Son to Read Doesn't Always Involve Books

Chapter 12 – Screen Time: The Good, the Bad, and the Ugly

Chapter 13 – Out of the Box Learning for Out of the Box Learners

Part Four: The Teacher

Chapter 14 - Learning to Ignore "Grade Level"

Chapter 15 - Just Because It is Difficult, Doesn't Mean You Are Doing It Wrong

Chapter 16 - The Lies I Believe About Being a "Special Needs" Mom

Chapter 17 - Dear Me, Here's Some Chocolate

Part One: "Special" Education

"The best teachers are those who show you where to look, but don't tell you what to see." - Alexandra K. Trenfor

Chapter 1: Our Story

When I was a little girl, I wanted to be a teacher.

I loved the idea of directing a classroom. I wanted to be the one behind the desk, grading papers. I wanted to have children hug my legs and give me apples. I wanted to write on chalkboards, create seasonally themed bulletin boards, and administer spelling tests.

When I was twenty years old, I found myself beginning the student teaching process. **I was now an Education major at the university, with an emphasis in Special Education.** I had completed all of my in-class preparation, and it was time to student teach - to put into practice all I had learned. I arrived early, on my very first day in that first grade classroom, feeling confident and excited.

I left that day certain that I had made a mistake. Teaching was a lot less about me than I had imagined. Teaching I quickly learned, was about the students and their needs. And the needs in that little classroom were so numerous, I felt I simply couldn't keep up.

My heart felt like it was breaking all day long, because I couldn't give the children the time and attention they required.

My education degree helped me become not a teacher, but a very successful training and development consultant. For ten years, I worked all over the country for various Fortune 500 companies, developing learning plans for employee development. After that, I worked with smaller businesses, defining business plans that leveraged people and their strengths as a business's #1 asset.

I was good at what I did, mostly **because** of my teaching background. Whereas businesses usually looked at operations and process first, I worked to help businesses see the potential that was right in front of them – their employees.

Time and time again, I saw businesses succeed against all odds, because of the attention they paid to individualized, employee development. I loved my job. I was well compensated. It was challenging work, and it required only my professional, logical side.

It did not require any part of my heart and honestly, I liked it that way.

Then, I became a mom.

Twice.

Two little boys that each stole a piece of my heart that I didn't know existed.

Two little boys that required more care than I ever thought I could possibly give.

I quit my job and pulled my oldest son out of public school at the end of second grade.

After two years, it was clear that although he was in the top 1% of second graders in the school district and had perfect grades, he was miserable *every single day* (and therefore so was I). It was also painfully clear that because he was so advanced academically, he was not learning anything new at all.

It took seeing him painfully try to fit in, hearing kids tease him about his 6th grade reading level, having meltdowns every morning over having to put on shoes/get out the door, his teacher telling me that she didn't need my input, the constant threat of bells ringing, crowded cafeterias, PE on the prickly grass…it took all of this to cause me to take a step back and say, **maybe this isn't working**.

Making the decision to homeschool was difficult for me. I went to school to be a teacher. I LOVED school myself.

But I also knew that my son and his little brother, were not loving it - not even a little. Their experiences seemed to be polar opposites of my own.

I saw their differences.

I heard the bullies making fun.

I felt the frustration of their teachers, trying to do the best they could for all 30 of their children, but not able to really devote too much time and attention to anyone.

After years of asking for help from doctors, teachers, and psychologists, to figure out why my children could not function in a mainstream classroom, we decided to eliminate the classroom. My youngest son finished preschool, but never saw the inside of a kindergarten classroom. My oldest packed up his desk on the last day of second grade and never returned.

A year later, my oldest son was diagnosed with autism and generalized anxiety disorder. He also scored in the genius range on his IQ test. It all began to make sense.

A year after that, we learned that my youngest son is profoundly dyslexic and has a significant processing delay. He too, scored in the genius range on the IQ test. More pieces of our education puzzle began to fall into place.

Two years later, we found ourselves back in a doctor's office, this time receiving two chronic illness diagnoses for my oldest son. Lupus and Sjogren's syndrome have completed our sons' list of unique circumstances that require special care.

Autism

Giftedness/Twice Exceptional

Dyslexia

Processing Delays

Chronic Illness

Ironically, almost all of the children in that first classroom I found myself student teaching in twenty years ago, fell into one or more of these diagnostic categories.

It is abundantly clear that God has been preparing me to be a special education teacher all along.

This book is about what I have learned, all along the way.

Chapter 2: Why "Special" Education?

When we hear the term "special ed" applied to our children it can be difficult. There is a stigma, whether we like it or not, associated with the entire concept.

But as a former "Special Education" professional, please allow me to explain why I don't shy away from it.

Special education might better be described as **Specialized Education**. The foundation of any special education program is simply that the student requires a more individualized approach, than a typical educational environment can provide.

And after working with many students over the years, and especially now that I have worked directly with my own children, I can tell you that a **special education is a gift to ANY learner.**

The key tenents of any special education program include Individualized Education Plans (IEP's), a team of experts, much smaller class sizes allowing for more one on one interaction, an explicit commitment to key resources for learning, and identifying milestones that measure success.

There is not a child alive that would not benefit from this type of intention and focus in their education.

I have found that the more I learn about homeschooling, the more I see that it could technically fall under the heading of "Special Education" and for all the right reasons!

Providing our children a special education is nothing to be ashamed of. I use the term intentionally and with great respect – it is after all in the title of this book!

I want to encourage you as we get started to allow yourself the freedom to ignore the stigma attached to the words themselves, and instead think about how the basic tenets can apply to your homeschool and your child.

Part Two: The Reality

"Little things are indeed little, but to be faithful in little things is a great thing." - Mother Teresa

Chapter 3: Am I Qualified to Homeschool My Child with Special Needs?

"Aren't you worried that you are keeping him from really getting the help he needs?"

"You don't want your son to miss out on the professional help the school system provides."

"How can you possibly think that you are more qualified than someone who has been trained to help with autism and dyslexia?"

All three of these comments were made by other moms, concerned about my ability to appropriately homeschool my boys.

All three caused me a little bit of anxiety. A little bit of fear. And then a whole lot of I just wish they could see how good this has been for my boys, how much progress they've made, how much this adds to their life *(and to mine)*.

We have been homeschooling now for more than five years. We began **before we had a single diagnosis for either child**. After two years in public school classrooms, it was clear that although he was in the top 1% of second graders in the school district and had perfect grades, my son was miserable *every single day*. Because he was so advanced academically, he was also not learning anything new at all.

The **sensory issues my son deals with every day**, are alone enough to make schooling at home a good choice for him. He could hear other student's pencils writing on papers in classrooms, the whir of the air conditioner, the ticking of the clock. He could smell the sickly, sweet lunch boxes in the corner after lunch, the grass on the bottom of someone's shoe, the markers used on the dry erase board. My son's memories of school mostly revolve around the sensory overload he experienced every single day.

It was a year after we began homeschooling, that he was finally diagnosed with autism and generalized anxiety disorder. As you know, a year later, we learned that **his brother is profoundly dyslexic.**

In both instances, I was asked if, now that we had the diagnoses, I would be putting the boys back in school.

My answer was a very resolved, "No."

One of the reasons I am so passionate about writing about homeschooling, is because I think there is a serious misconception that homeschooling not a viable option when your child has special needs. Moreover, there is also a perception that a child with special needs is missing out on valuable therapies and resources, when they are not a part of the school system.

The question I am most often asked in relationship to homeschooling with special needs is this -

Am I Qualified to Homeschool My Children with Special Needs?

My answer is, in short, "Yes."

1. I do have some training.
   As you know, I actually went to school to be a special education teacher back in the day. I did my student teaching in special education classrooms. I studied book upon book about individualized learning plans, IEP's, education law, and classroom management. As a result, I know a little more than some about what my children could expect in a special needs classroom. I also know that for my two guys, there is no way that would be an option. **Both of my children have genius level IQ's, but also have serious education deficits.** This asynchrony (also called 'twice exceptional') makes classroom

placement difficult. For example, at home, my dyslexic nine-year old is reading at a 1st to 2nd grade level, but is completing 7th grade level science and history. This would be impossible to replicate in a school environment. *(Please note: In my state, no special training or education level is required at all to homeschool any child, including those with special needs. Some states do require a little more oversight, but all allow parents to choose to homeschool their children, no matter what the diagnosis. I have some education and training, but it is not necessary or required.)*

2. My children do have **access to therapists and use outside resources** *(boy do they)*. My youngest saw an educational therapist for a year to help lay the groundwork for reading. In addition, I met with her once a month and she taught me the methods she used with him, so that I could replicate them at

home. The same is true for occupational therapy and social skills therapies for my oldest. We are by no means doing this alone, and have plenty of experts helping to speak into my children's overall development.

3. **Every single mom I know with unique little ones like mine is an expert.**
I say this with complete confidence. We read more books, learn more online, ask more questions and try to piece together answers for our children beyond what the school system can provide. **Children with special needs, whether in school or not, rely on their parents to be their most passionate advocates.** This is true in IEP meetings, doctors' appointments, therapists' offices and parent teacher conferences, without fail. It is also true in homeschooling. I know my boys better than anyone else on the planet. I know what works and what doesn't work when my oldest did not sleep and was anxious all night long. I know how difficult the last

set of sight words were for my youngest, and can take the time to research the best way to help him proceed. I have the time and the passion that would be unrealistic to expect from anyone else. You do too.

4. This is the Best Choice for my Family

I care deeply about my children's education. I have put a lot of thought into this. What I have found is that homeschooling is the best way to give them what they need to be successful in life. This is true academically, as well as socially. We have a supportive and loving community of friends who also homeschool. My children benefit from the opportunity to make friends in their own time and at their own pace, as much as they benefit from progressing academically at their own pace. Homeschooling actually gives them a social experience that makes sense for their needs.

The longer we do this, the more progress I see, and the more I learn that **I am perfectly qualified to homeschool my children with special needs.**

So are you.

And I am grateful we have the opportunity to do so.

Chapter 4: Getting Started

My first day of homeschooling was amazing. The second day was positively awful. Every day since has been somewhere in between.

And so it goes....

I was over-prepared for all the wrong things, when we began homeschooling. The bookshelves were tidy, the curriculum was perfectly planned, and the crafts were ready to go that first day.

What I lacked was perspective.

I spent most of that first year frustrated and tired. We were headed towards a diagnosis, I knew it at that point, but I still found myself trying to re-create the very school environment that had been such a disaster for my children.

Getting started was daunting. I wanted to quit more times than I could count. I hid in the bathroom and cried big tears more days than not. **To this day, I am still 100% sure that I am messing this thing up.**

Five years later though, I can tell you that it has all been worth it.

Here is what I wish someone would have said to me, as we were getting started.

> #1 - *You are not alone in doubting your abilities.*
>
> #2 - **Make Learning About Your Children Your First Priority**

You Are Not Alone in Doubting Your Abilities

If you have considered this option for your child, but are worried that you won't be able to do it well, you are not alone. Every single momma I know who homeschools her children has exactly this same fear. *And every single one of their children, are learning and thriving.*

Like anything else with our children, there are some things we just have to figure out as we go. Homeschooling is like that, only with field trips and clay.

Make Learning About Your Children Your First Priority

This will save you so much time, effort and frustration. I made the mistake initially, of thinking that my boys would need to get used to me being their teacher. I was wrong. I found that in order to really be able to accommodate their unique needs, I needed to learn as much as possible about them!

Here are some examples of what I have come to know about my children, and now this information informs our homeschooling.

1. For My Youngest Son, Slow is Fast.

My youngest is nine. He processes information about 30% slower than the average bear and has profound learning differences that affect his ability to read, spell and write. He also happens to be highly gifted and have reasoning abilities that were off the charts in his evaluation. These unique qualities now color almost everything I do in educating him, particularly how I pace his learning.

For example, he is still not able to spell, or even consistently read the word "the". We have been working on memorizing this small, but I am sure you would agree, very important word in the English language for almost three full years now. We have done flash cards, written copy work, spelled with blocks, numerous worksheets, countless read alouds, and even made up our own song (*t-h-e spells "the"*). He still doesn't recognize it right away most of the time. You can imagine that this can be frustrating, and it is – both for me and especially for him. My son knows he should know it, but he just can't retrieve the information from his complicated little brain.

In his case, slower is better. In the long run it is actually *faster*.

Trying to force him to "get it", or just skipping to the next topic because I just can't take reviewing the same thing, again and again, in the long run means he learns less. I have found that praying for patience, trying to find a new approach (*Honey, let's write the word "the" in shaving cream over and over again on the shower wall today*), and just accepting that this is the speed that is right for him, allows him to progress, at his pace, in a meaningful way.

Conversely, the other day he solved one of his older brother's math word problems *in his head*. When things are read aloud, and he can just focus on the details of an equation or a problem to be solved, he is ridiculously brilliant. So, I read everything to him. His math book, his science lesson, history, Harry Potter books, books about animals, the scientific method and how to build perfect paper airplanes. He recently picked up a book about Leonardo da Vinci (who is it rumored was dyslexic himself) and asked me to read it to him. He then proceeded to discuss the more complicated aspects of the machines good old Leo designed. He can pick up the information quickly, but it requires a ton of time to carefully read every single thing to him, all day long. It works because again, although it may seem slow to me, he learns rapidly and beyond grade level with this approach.

2. For my Oldest Son, More is More.

My two boys could not be more different. As I said above, for my youngest, less information is better. For my twelve-year-old, there are not enough books on the planet to keep him occupied and learning. An exceptionally fast reader, he retains more detailed information from what he reads, than seems possible for a human being that is not also half computer. He collects and categorizes information as if there is a Dewey Decimal system in his brain. He reads, on average, between 30-45 books a month (not joking and yes, that is more than one per day), most of them non-fiction. He can tell you almost anything you want to know about chemistry, every single detail of Greek Mythology, The Revolutionary War, WWII, and even parts of nuclear physics. He knows just about the entire world map, including every country, most major cities and even key exports/notable historic moments in various areas of the world. He knows all of this, because we allow him to focus almost all of his school day on reading (*devouring*) books and talking with him about them.

The two things he struggles with most, are holding a pencil and math.

Holding a pencil is a very big deal for my son. Because his hands are such an affected part of his sensory processing disorder, it is extremely uncomfortable for him to write anything – even to practice signing his name. I allow him to type just about everything, but part of his school day includes an attempt at practicing signing his name, as if he needed to write a check or secure a contract. I say "attempt" because some days, this is just too much for him and he literally cannot do it no matter how hard he tries. I try not to freak out about his future (*where I imagine him making X's on all legal documents*), and he does his best to practice on days when he is feeling better.

Math has also been a struggle – largely because it is difficult to learn math through simply reading and accumulating information. What has been helpful for us is including the second set of books in a series called "Life of Fred". These books tell a story and incorporate advanced math into the plot as a way to learn concepts. Sourdough learns very well this way, and has started giving me algebraic equations to solve while we drive. (*He can now easily do algebra, but still has to use a calculator for basic multiplication – ah the joys of asynchronous learning.*) We also practice with math drills and worksheets, but I do the writing for him.

Paying close attention to what naturally works and what does not work, allows me to better educate my children. It also makes learning much more fun, and me a lot less stressed.

If you are just getting started, please let me encourage you.

You can do this.

Let your child teach you how he needs to learn.

And one more time, you can do this.

Chapter 5: Expectations vs. Reality

"I think you might be losing sight of the fact that he has an autism spectrum diagnosis. That's not going away. We need to talk about adjusting your expectations."

This is what the behavioral pediatrician told me in our appointment last week.

She said it in response to me telling her all the things we were "working on" and all the things that were not going well and all the meltdowns that we wish weren't part of our life.

Last week was not a great one.

I started off feeling totally overwhelmed by what I perceived as the lack of progress in our life. My son's sensory system was a jangled mess and his younger brother not reading the word "the" (*again*) was enough to make me want to go back to bed.

Add to that a major meltdown that erupted in actual punches being thrown at his brother *in the post office*, plus the lady with way too much make-up that made a very rude comment, and **I was certain I had completely failed us - again.** I went to bed praying for direction and order and peace. The next day, we had a follow-up appointment with his developmental pediatrician.

God has perfect timing.

When the doctor asked my son to leave the room, I thought she was going to tell me all the things we needed to do next. Instead, **she basically said my expectations don't match my reality.**

My son has Autism.

He has severe sensory processing issues that aggravate an already pervasive anxiety disorder.

He will have meltdowns. Period.

He will perseverate on topics for days and weeks at a time. Period.

He will struggle with his body and balance and social function. Period.

Apparently, I am still struggling to fully accept all of this. Apparently, I still need the doctor to confirm a diagnosis that I can so plainly see right in front of me.

And her doing so was an absolute blessing. I walked out of her office in tears...tears of relief and gratitude.

I spent the rest of the week focused on how best to help and love and accept my son, right where he is.

Actually, I spent the rest of the week focused on how best to help and love and accept my life, right where it is.

Expectations, ones that do not match my reality, are suffocating.

Maybe you have encountered this as well?

The should's.

The what-if's.

The why is this not getting any better's.

Please don't misunderstand, we should work to make progress. And I was reminded that we have made progress, *a ton*.

When I first walked into that office, I was terrified. My son hadn't slept in weeks.

He was harming himself, and me, every single day.

I had forgotten how far we've come.

When my expectations don't match my reality, we all lose.

Expectations are like that - **I get so focused on how I think things should be, that I lose sight of how wonderful they already are.**

One year later, he sleeps all the way through the night (*well, most of the time*). We can actually leave the house and not worry about someone getting hurt in the car. He hasn't hurt himself in months. He hasn't hurt me in even longer.

If you had told me a year ago that our current reality is what I could look forward to, I would've rejoiced and cried tears of joy.

Finally, brothers, whatever is true, whatever is honorable, whatever is just, whatever is pure, whatever is lovely, whatever is commendable, if there is any excellence, if there is anything worthy of praise, think about these things.
Philippians 4:8

Our reality is worthy of excellence and praise. So much is lovely and commendable and true.

Rather than unrealistic, defeating expectations, I will think about these things.

Two beautiful sons.

A wonderful husband.

Diagnoses that help us know what to do to help.

Therapists that love my boys and genuinely want to invest in them.

A loaf of fresh-baked bread that my little guy helped make.

Spelling the word "the" correctly in today's school work.

A wonderful book.

The sound of birds chirping in the morning.

Our backyard.

Picking tomatoes.

My son telling me he loves me, without any prompting.

Friends that text me a serious, deep thought and a joke with emoticons all in the same sentence.

A gentle, loving reminder that this is the life, the only life, I have been given.

Prayers whispered, "May I live it well."

May you live it well.

Chapter 6: Sleep Matters

This morning was a tough one.

I was up until almost 4:00 AM with my son. In the haze of perseverating chatter about computer builds and salt water tanks, I was struck at around 3:00 AM, at how little my life has changed. It's been 13 years since my son was a newborn, and yet many nights feel exactly the same.

Sleeping for short stretches, only to be awakened by the needs of a child I love dearly – but just is not equipped to sleep – is a constant in my life.

Mothering a child with special needs can be so, so tiring. Literally. So tiring.

Studies suggest that nearly 80% of children with autism and other special needs have sleep problems. This means that 80% of parents with children with autism and other special needs also have sleep problems. It is a very real, very present reality for many of us.

And, in my experience, one that most doctors and therapists cannot really identify with. "Make sure you cut out any sugar and electronics for at least three hours before bedtime," was the constant recommendation when my son was younger. It was infuriating. We had been doing that for years, with absolutely no effect.

Sleeping for very short periods of time, only to be wakened again and again is used as torture in some countries. I for one, would like to say I understand why.

And my son is just as tired. The years of not sleeping well take their toll.

One of the greatest benefits of homeschooling for us has been the ability to accommodate sleep disturbances.

If my youngest son is anxious until 2:30 AM, I can allow him to sleep in a bit the next morning instead of waking him for the 7:30 AM bus.

If my oldest wakes for the day at 3:30 AM, I can change our plan for the day to include more relaxed and less strenuous activities and learning.

If both of them are awake off and on all night (and they often are), I can choose to turn on documentaries and take a nap on the couch for a few hours in the afternoon.

This may seem basic, and I guess it is. But it's true.

Sleep, and the lack there of, makes a significant difference in our children's ability to learn and retain information. Working with my sons' natural sleep patterns, instead of constantly fighting against them has lessened the constant stress bedtimes and wake times once caused us.

If your family struggles with consistent sleep, like mine, I want to encourage you to view accommodating your child's sleep needs as part of your family's homeschool plan.

Chapter 7: Life Skills

My son showed me exactly how he planned to install a CPU into his computer yesterday.

(If you don't know what that is, don't worry. You are in good company. I listen to my son tell me all about computer parts for most of the day, every day, and I am still not 100% sure I know what it really is.)

He walked me through step by step, in painstaking detail, not only how to install it, but how the actual device functions. The way it communicates, what one set of cords does vs. the other, why the motherboard goes in this spot, and so many more things that I completely did not understand a single word of.

I sat there in awe, so proud of the man he is becoming. He is realizing his strengths, and using them to compensate for the aspects of his life that are difficult.

It is exactly what he has been working towards for almost four years now.

And, I couldn't help but feel a pang of confusion and disbelief.

He can do all of this.

But he may not be able to navigate dinner tonight.

It's something I don't think we talk about as much as we should. A child on the autism spectrum often masters things are that outrageously difficult for a NT individual - sometimes even impossible (never being taught to build a computer, and yet being able to do just that is a small example).

But it's the basics that are difficult.

Eating.

Sleeping.

Drinking Water.

Shopping.

Taking Medicines.

Showering.

Getting Dressed.

Playing.

These are the areas of my son's life that are the most complicated.

They are also the areas of my mothering that are the most challenging.

They happen every single day, all day. Eating and sleeping are basic life requirements, and yet they are, without a doubt, the most challenging aspects of my son's life.

"I'm hungry, but I can't eat."

"I'm tired, but I can't sleep."

"I want to go to the store and look at air fresheners, but I can't be in the store."

He has learned to better communicate what is happening. And it's so helpful. Verbally being able to say I can't do something is a big deal around here.

And I am grateful for it.

And it is exhausting.

Here is an average day mothering my son through the basics of his life:

Morning

He didn't want breakfast at 9:00 AM. It's now 10:00 AM. Time to try again.

Nope. OK. I will ask again at 10:30 AM and this time I will offer bagels and cream cheese. That's soft, it might work.

Good, bagels and cream cheese it is. Except, no. He took one bite and gagged.

OK, scrambled eggs worked. Now we can get his medicines prepped.

He said he would take them in an hour - he just can't right now with the taste of egg in his mouth. I need to set an alarm so I don't forget.

11:45 AM and meds are down.

Afternoon

It's 2:00 PM and he wants to go to the pet store. I need him to eat something first. The pet store is usually OK, but the lighting and smells can be weird, and we have had meltdowns there before.

Deep breath.

It's 2:30 PM and I am making a turkey sandwich. One of his favorites. We should be good to go.

Evening

It's dinner time and he wants to eat in his room again. There are studies that show families that eat at the table together do well. But he hates the feeling of the chair on his hip. And he can't stand the sound of his brother chewing, or tapping his feet on the floor, or both.

Am I a bad mom for just letting him eat the flippin' lasagna alone? At least he is eating. I am going to let it go.

We are getting close to bedtime and I am thinking through how to help him shower. The smell of teenage boy is real. I know it's tough for him, but we gotta do it.

He balks. Shoot.

I decide to entice him with the brand new items we bought at Lush. Maybe the shower gel will be my friend right now.

He is seriously not going to do it. He says it is just too much tonight and that he promises to shower tomorrow. I decide to respect his wishes. He is communicating how he feels. That is progress.

We have nothing planned outside of our house tomorrow. It should be calmer. He should be able to keep that promise.

The Middle of the Night

It's 1:30 AM and he is still up. He wants to sleep. It's obvious that he is tired. But he just can't. I ask him if he wants to talk to me a little, just to get drowsy.

He does.

I feel my eyelids closing every once in a while, but for the most part, I am pleased that he is so calm. Instead of getting anxious he is settling down.

By 2:15 AM, he is asleep. By 2:16 AM, so am I.

Our life necessarily looks different. My son spends more time learning the basics, like eating and hygiene, than he ever will in subjects like science and math.

And I am 100% OK with it.

What makes it complicated is the rest of the world. Not understanding, assuming he is spoiled, questioning why I allow him to make the decision instead of just demanding obedience. Too often, my son is questioned as to why he just can't take the meds, eat the foods, go to the store.

By doctors. By other kids. By his brother.

He doesn't have an answer to that question. If he did, we wouldn't be spending so much time on these things.

And, too often, I am also questioned. By the well-meaning specialist, by a mom who doesn't know us very well, by my youngest son.

But I have an answer.

Everyone is different. Everyone has strengths and weaknesses. My son is stronger in his strengths than any 13-year-old I know. He also works harder, every single day, on the things that are tough for him.

Sometimes the basics are the most difficult.

Sometimes simple, isn't simple. Sometimes development looks wildly different for one child vs. another. And sometimes, we just have to proceed at the pace that is right for our children. Homeschool allows us to do just that.

I don't think the basics will ever be easy for my son. But I have seen enough progress to know that he will eventually figure out how to best approach eating, sleeping and shopping.

Until then, I will help him. We will incorporate life skills into our days as if they were an algebra class or language arts program.

Homeschooling allows me to really help him in the areas he needs it most.

It's a basic premise, but one that I think we often overlook as parents homeschooling children with special needs.

Please let me encourage you – many special education programs in traditional schools often incorporate life skills such as grocery shopping, cooking, and navigating bus schedules. You are doing the exact same thing when you are working with your little one on brushing her teeth.

It counts. Not only as parenting, but as education.

Part Three: The Learning

"ABC. Easy as One, two, three. Or simple as Do re mi, ABC, one, two, three, baby, you and me." - Jackson 5

Chapter 8: Feeling the Pressure to Recreate School

I had a school room with a lovely, perfectly organized set of books, curriculum, and manipulatives. I had a bell, all set and ready to ring for start time, break time, and lunch time.

It was going to be amazing.

And it was.

For exactly one day.

Then reality of homeschooling hit. My children did not do well in a school environment. It was one of the reasons they were no longer going to school. So why was I trying to recreate that exact environment in our home?

There are so many ways that this has played out in the past five years:

- Like the time **I was convinced that my sons needed to be in classes at least one day a week, so that they could be social and learn from a better teacher than me.** (Let me just repeat what I already wrote: *A school environment did not work well for my children. It was obvious. But I am a slow learner, and apparently really like spending money on registration fees and classes that we will only attend for approximately two weeks until I remember why we pulled them out of school and homeschool in the first place.*)

- Or the time **I thought I really needed to add knitting and crochet to our curriculum.** (Because that is what every prepubescent, special needs child needs – to try desperately to complete a fine motor skill task that even his mom can't do.)
- Or the time **I was sure that if we started school every day by 8:30 a.m., we would somehow be more focused and actually learn all the things.**

I am sad to say that the person who has learned the most in this homeschooling journey, especially when it comes to helping my children academically, is me.

Recreating a school environment just doesn't work for my children. Maybe it doesn't for yours either.

What I have learned is that it matters so much less than I thought.

This book is about what I have learned to do instead...

Chapter 9: Embracing the Actual vs. the Idea of How it Would Be

"If they would just _____."

(Fill in the blank here: wake up earlier, do what I am asking them, not be so resistant, sit still for a few minutes, let me read the lovely read-aloud, not ask me seven times for a snack, just complete the math worksheet so we can move on, etc., etc., etc.)

Too often, I think if they would just be the learners I want them to be, instead of the ones that they actually are, I would be an amazing homeschooling mom.

And it helps no one. Because the truth is, this has nothing to do with me being amazing.

It has nothing to do with my children doing what all of the other homeschool kids seemingly do so well.

I have learned that challenging my children academically, **is about helping them learn in the ways that actually work.**

It is about helping them feel confident and excited about the world around them, despite their special needs and the barriers they face in that world.

This is about ditching my expectations of how homeschooling should be, and instead leaning in to what it actually is for us: audiobooks in the car, spelling tests in Minecraft, YouTube videos in bed on a sick day, heading to the park and letting my son move and play while I read aloud, and writing stories on the windows with washable markers.

None of this is how I think it "should" be. None of this matches the picture I have in my head. And yet all of this is how my children learn best.

The more I embrace the creative, out of the box, never a dull moment boys that I have been given, the easier this homeschool gig becomes.

They learn more. They enjoy my company, and I theirs. They engage in the world. They are excited to learn.

And that matches my expectations for our homeschool perfectly.

Chapter 10: Learning Everywhere BUT Home

My oldest son, who has autism, was also recently diagnosed with an autoimmune disease that causes chronic pain and fatigue.

My youngest son, is getting older. He is profoundly dyslexic, and I am finding that as he matures, he is also profoundly incapable of learning unless it involves moving, jumping, spinning and/or hanging upside down.

The more we move through this wonderfully messy life, the more I am realizing that our homeschool is not going to look like anyone else's that I know, or the ones in many of the blogs or books I read.

For example, last week we had a series of doctors' appointments that not only meant we were at the hospital for the entire day, but we had a two hour drive to get there and back.

And in a fit of desperation, we ended up at the local fish store (again), because my oldest is completely obsessed with aquariums right now.

And my youngest wants nothing to do with books, but thinks the skate park and his friend's backyard might be his second homes.

I find that as I try and meet the needs of my ever changing family, we have been homeschooling at home less and less.

At first, I totally rebelled. I was sure if it wasn't at home and part our routine for the day, then it didn't really "count" as learning.

I tried and I tried on the days we were at home, to make up for lost time. In what might be the largest understatement I have ever typed, please allow me to say – *it did not work.* Not. At. All.

The more I pushed, the more stress we all felt. The more stress we all felt, the more emotions flared. The more emotions flared, the less anyone really ended up learning.

As we approached the end of the school year, I decided it was time to just let it go. I gave up and did the best I could, with the reality of our new, more hectic schedule.

Our learning consisted mostly of:

Carschooling

I didn't know this was an actual term until this year, but let me say, it has changed my life.

Audio books in the car, when no one was really listening to the read aloud on the couch.

Learning apps on the iPad including, 'Stack the States' and 'Presidents vs. Zombies', when our US history curriculum was falling woefully behind.

Google searches using the smart phone when a random question about native birds comes up (prompted only by daydreaming and looking out the window on a long drive).

All have served our learning very, very well.

(That and we get from point A to point B without arguments, the repetitive "I'm bored," or meltdowns. Please say it with me – Win Win!)

Local Businesses

My son's complete fixation on fish and aquariums meant we were at a fish and/or pet store at least three times last week (and four times the week before).

The crazy thing is, I cannot believe how much we learned in our time there.

Sometimes, my son would educate his younger brother about coral reefs or the difference between fresh water rivers in South America vs. Africa.

Sometimes, the shop owner would take pity on me and take over, discussing care and the operational aspects of tank ownership.

Most of the time, we just wandered, and both of my sons would talk non-stop about all the new things they had learned about this fish and that habitat.

When the fourth customer mentioned to me how smart my boys were, I decided to just relax and enjoy the time as a different opportunity to learn.

Playdates

As our *not at home at all schedule* has intensified, I have been tempted to eliminate the playdates on our calendar, and just stay home for a change.

I am so glad I didn't.

Every time my boys are with their friends, I am encouraged to see how much they are developing – and not just socially.

Often, a playdate will consist of cooking projects, building things, recording videos, and telling stories. I was struck a few weeks ago by how much our playdate looked like a small school, with age appropriate projects going on all around us.

We homeschool, but often not at home. I have struggled for years to accept that this "counts" as school.

And yet, they continue to improve and make progress academically.

It counts, as much as any workbook or more traditional classroom activity.

It's what they learn that matters more than how.

Chapter 11: Teaching My Dyslexic Son to Read Does Not Always Involve Books

My youngest son is nine years old. He is technically in the third grade. He loves animals, building structures in the woods, and jumping on our trampoline as often as possible. He can do complex math in his head, complete entire science experiments on his own, and knows more about World Geography than I do.

He is also unable to read even the most basic book.

He shies away from any activity that he thinks might possibly have anything to do with reading, including Sunday School, homeschool co-op classes, and has even asked me not to read aloud to him anymore at night.

My son has repeatedly said, over and over again, that he wants to learn to read, but not with books.

I believe my response has always been something like, "No way Jose. We love books in this family. You have to learn to read with books."

My son is profoundly dyslexic. He wants to read – desperately. He has been asking for years to learn. **This is not about reluctance. It is about his brain's ability to decipher and comprehend the code we call the English language.**

And the more he has tried and failed, the more I have researched and read books about dyslexia, and the more I have freaked out and pushed harder.

One day, as his reading lesson once again went down the path of tears, resistance, anger and frustration, I sent my son to his room to calm down. I sighed to myself and looked down at the page he had been struggling to get through in the story book that accompanies our curriculum.

The sentences in this book were essentially along the lines of, "The six foxes jump."

He is nine. He can name half the elements on the periodic table, and has regularly told me all about how he would survive in the Amazon

Rain Forest. (Between you and me, he probably could).

It struck me in that moment that my child has interests, and on some level maturity, way beyond the books we were using to help him learn to fluidly read.

It also struck me that he never resisted learning when we were using other tools (i.e. flashcards, air writing, 3D letters, etc). It was only when we pulled out the really basic primers that he lost his mind and quit.

Could he really be on to something?

What if I allowed him to learn to read without the books themselves? Would he gain back his natural joy and curiosity about reading? More importantly, would he actually learn to read?

Although everything in my heart screamed, "No way!" I decided to give it a try.

Here is what our new lessons in "reading" look like:

1. We read, but not for "reading."

Although we still read books, I read them aloud and they are not part of our dedicated time for "reading" lessons. They are books about historic figures, and age-appropriate chapter books that he enjoys.

What I love is that he no longer associates books with pain and frustration.

We also use wordless books. He creates stories to go along with the pictures, and he narrates them to me, using age appropriate sentence structure and vocabulary. Finally, audio books remain a regular part of his routine.

2. We use the trampoline.

We draw words on the trampoline in sidewalk chalk and he jumps to them on my prompt. We practice sight words and create sentences, without so much as a book jacket or pencil in sight.

Sometimes, when reading practice is over, I will climb in with him and complete the rest of the day's learning. (He thinks it is more fun sitting on the trampoline. I think it is more fun to get it done without fuss and before 1 p.m., so it works.)

3. We modify the curriculum to be multi-sensory.

Because repetition and consistency are so important in helping the dyslexic child learn to read, we still use our [All About Reading curriculum](#), but I modify it to allow for greater flexibility.

For instance, in practicing the program's sight words, he will often say and spell the word, then tap out the letters or sounds on his forearm, then "air write" the word, and finally write the word in his notebook.

We incorporate my son's interests for practice.

My son loves Minecraft. He LOVES it.

Did I mention he loves it?

There are signs that one can create in Minecraft – like a blank sheet of adolescent approved paper. He asked me one day to help him write out a sentence (this never, ever happened before.)

Once I realized this was an option, I decide to try and put it to good use. Now, as part of his learning, I write out a word or sentence, and he then inputs it into the Minecraft screen.

Every day, we go through the signs he has created, and he practices reading the sentences. Some of them are the ones he came up with, and others are the ones I suggest (which also happen to be from the <u>All About Reading</u> practice list).

Please smile with me and say "Win-Win!"

5. We are working our way back to actual books.

I know I will need to help my son move back into practicing reading fluency. Whether he likes it or not, the best way to do this is with books.

In trying to be intentional about this goal, I have started to read him age-appropriate, fun books in which he is genuinely interested.

What he doesn't know is that these books are on the reading level just above where he is currently performing. **I imagine a day, in the not too distant future, when he will be able to read these same books aloud to me, without fear, shame, and frustration.**

These changes have not required all that much (I am so happy to say). Our day-to-day learning is actually easier for me, now that he is not fighting it.

More importantly, although I did not think it possible, my son has made more progress in the last couple months, than in years prior.

Most importantly, he now has a sense of control (small and measured, but control just the same) over how he learns to read.

It has been a learning curve for both of us, but the results have been so encouraging. There is more learning here than ever before.

Slowly but surely, he learning to read and understand written language.

Chapter 12: Screen Time – The Good, the Bad, and the Ugly

This week that I am writing this chapter happens to be "Screen-Free" week.

Or around here, *"Feel Like A Bad Mom"* week.

When I think about the amount of time my children spend on screens, my head hurts.

The guilt.

The assurance that I am absolutely doing the wrong thing.

The feeling that good mommas would never...

The truth is, I sometimes hate screen time. I see the effect it has been known to have on my children and others. I also see the effect that getting outside, being in nature, and just moving has on my children and others.

So why do I allow it, more than what I have come to know is more than the average mom?

Because the truth is, **there are real, very tangible benefits to "screen time" that matter more to me than the detriments.**

I know this is not a popular, or even widely held view. In fact, I am a little nervous to even include this chapter in my book.

But every year, the ever lovin' "Screen Free Week" happens, and every year I freak out about it, feel guilty, and we fail the screen free test miserably.

This year, I have decided instead, to acknowledge and intentionally define why our family has chosen a different screen time path.

1. My family has unique educational needs that make screen time a fabulous tool.

I have two sons, ages 13 and 10.

As you now well know, my oldest son has autism and massive anxiety that is exacerbated by sensory processing issues. *The best way for him to learn anything is in complete silence. Even the sound of another person's pencil on a piece of paper is enough to cause major stress and drama.*

Even my voice can ring in his ears after just a very short lesson.

But watching a quick You-Tube video on Peru for example, and then finding various websites to research and learn? This has made my son a serious expert in all things Peruvian, including native plants, animals, topography, geography, the different cultures within Peru, travel and tourism, and more.

Because he could do it at his own pace, and in a way that works well with his sensory needs, the iPad acted as his primary teacher for all of this, with me merely checking in from time to time to see how he is doing. His sixth grade country report is wonderful, and by the way, he completed the report in PowerPoint, without my help. Yet another screen, yet another advantage for him.

This same child also has an auto-immune disorder that creates massive joint and nerve pain, making him sometimes so fatigued that he literally cannot get out of bed. On the bad days, he still completes some "learning". I lie down with him, and we watch You-Tube videos together. Is it ideal? No. But it keeps him engaged on days that are so very tough for him, physically and emotionally.

My youngest son, of course, has a different set of educational needs. He has profound dyslexia and a processing disorder. He is on the screens much less, but mostly because he is naturally a very active child. He enjoys everything about the outdoors and given the choice, would much rather put down the iPad, and go out and bounce on the trampoline.

Still, Minecraft has been a very effective tool to help him with spelling and reading. We use it to practice typing sentences and commands. He thinks he is merely playing a game, and I see the progress he makes when he is not so anxious about his lack of reading ability.

For my youngest, I find I am actually *intentionally* finding ways to incorporate screens into his learning. Educational apps and learning games are age appropriate for my ten-year-old barely reading at a second grade level. Books are still a part of his learning, of course, but as I have mentioned, most in his reading level are babyish and dull. They cause so much more self-doubt and anxiety than any screen ever could.

2. There are very few people who can easily babysit my boys.

So this is a selfish benefit, but a screen time benefit just the same.

With my children's unique needs, there are only a handful of people we know can handle them well. And when we do get someone to watch them, it's so we can go out for the evening, or get much-needed errands done.

The truth is, sometimes, screens help me get the laundry folded in peace.

Sometimes, they keep my youngest safe and distracted when his older brother is violently melting down.

Sometimes, they let me take a quick nap when I have been up since 3:30 in the morning with an anxiety ridden child.

It's not ideal, but it works and *we are all better because of it.*

3. We do have limits, but on when to take breaks and on content, not overall time spent on the screen.

In our family, we have specific limits on content. We do not allow mature rated video games and often talk to our boys about not electronically training their minds to be violent.

We also do not allow them to speak and interact with each other any differently than they would while playing outside together. This includes language, not helping each other out, and name calling.

The boys can now recite my mantras – *'There May Be A Screen Between You, but Your Brother Is Still Your Brother On The Other Side'* and *'Real People Matter More Than The Electronic Ones'*.

We also encourage frequent and regular breaks. Similar to what I employed when I worked in an office setting, I plan for my sons to get up and get out regularly, thereby avoiding long stretches of screen time. Sometimes, they hurry through whatever task or outdoor activity I ask them to do. Other times, they get totally caught up in something else and do not return to the screen. Either way, this seems to dramatically lessen the wild hyperactivity or aggression that can sometimes occur from too much time spent staring at a screen.

When all is said and done, this is just what works for us. Every family is different, and I trust your decisions to be what is best for yours.

Clearly my children's needs are unique, but I think in any family, **being intentional about screen time can be just as beneficial as eliminating it all together.**

And with that, I must go.

I need to shut down *my* screen and prepare to make lemon bars with my son. He found the recipe on a YouTube channel and is looking forward to trying them.

Happy "**Screen Free**", or "**Screens Sometimes**", or "**Screens Gone Wild**" week to you and yours.

Chapter 13: Out of the Box Learning for Out of the Box Kids

"I neeeeeeeeed to move around while you are reading to me, Momma. It's how I listen," my youngest child said to me, spinning in circles as I tried to get him to sit down with me on the couch and pay attention.

My then six-year-old child, who clearly had more energy than the rest of our entire family combined, wasn't telling me something new. He wasn't telling me something I hadn't read in numerous books, blogs, and research studies. In fact, in college, I spent an entire semester studying how to teach deaf children to read using movement.

I have known for years that children, especially young children, often learn best when incorporating play and movement into their educational activities. And yet it took my little boy looking me square in the eye and begging me to *help him help me* teach, to actually start incorporating play into our learning.

Sometimes, I really am the student in this whole homeschooling thing.

Why does it seem so difficult to make play a part of learning? For me, it has been a direct result of these three things:

1. It's Less Measurable

The truth is, a worksheet or a structured "sit down at the table and follow the lesson plan" activity is easily measured. When it is complete, it's complete. We can check it off the list and move on to the next assignment. This is reassuring to me. It means I can "prove" my children have been "taught" something.

Yet the truth is, this approach is much more about me needing to feel successful than it is about them actually learning (Ouch...).

2. It Conflicts with My Own Learning Style

When I was a child, I was the one who truly enjoyed just sitting and reading a book. To this day, I am better able to focus if I can sit still. This is certainly not the case for my children, but I find myself falling back on my own version of how I think we should learn, over and over again.

3. It Requires Some Planning and Intentionality

Being able to pull off moving and play in conjunction with a lesson requires me to really think through how to modify the lesson. Because it requires extra planning, it is easier to just stick to the lesson plan as-is, instead of going rogue with our learning. It also often requires extra set-up (and clean-up for that matter!). So if I am already feeling behind or overwhelmed, play is often the first to go in our school routine.

Although these have been real challenges for me as a momma and teacher, my heart really is to provide an individualized, fun, and appropriate education for my boys. I know that movement and play help provide just that.

As time has gone on, through conversations with other mommas and just simply trial and error, I have learned a few tips that have helped incorporate more hands-on play and movement into our everyday learning.

Tip #1 – Messy is not a dirty word

I have learned to not base any educational lesson planning on how much mess there will be before and after the activity. I have two boys. The state of our bathroom has proven to me over and over again that our life will involve some mess. Why should our school be any different?

My children are so much more engaged and have so much more fun when they are able to complete hands-on projects, without me freaking out over every sticky, dirty, cluttered surface the project involves. More importantly, **they learn more**. They are better able to recall the information we discuss as they create and they connect that information to the three dimensional activity before them. I will take sticky floors if it means the learning "sticks" as well.

Tip #2 – Be Intentional and Plan for Play

For me, this looks different for each of my children. My youngest is super active, so I intentionally modify some activities to include movement. For example, when we are practicing speech sounds (as part of his speech therapy), I will say a letter and then kick a ball to him. He will make the sound associated with the letter and then kick the ball back to me. I have no idea why this works for him, but it does. When he is thinking about kicking the ball, he actually is better able to articulate the sound and remembers it better in the long run.

For my oldest, this looks very different. While movement is not necessarily essential for his attention and retention, talking through what he has learned is. (Note to momma: verbal processing = constant chatter about all the things.) In order to help incorporate a little more fun into his learning, we have started creating "How-To" videos. He scripts his video and then records himself "teaching" whatever it is that he has learned. He feels like it is "play" and I find it a great way to check his understanding before we move on to a new topic.

My oldest also struggles with sensory processing issues. The only way to really synch up his sensory system is to get him moving. Unlike his brother, this requires a lot more effort on his part, and mine. Completing "occupational therapy" at home has helped me incorporate movement into his days. Because OT has been a regular part of his life for so long, he understands it's benefits (or at the very least, knows it is not optional). For ten to twenty minutes every day, I incorporate some of his exercises from therapy into our learning.

An important element of this planning is paying attention to the unique gifts God has given each of my children. Then, I must be intentional about using those gifts in our learning. Play allows me to tailor our generic lessons to how each of my boys best function and succeed.

Tip #3 – Movement does not always mean lack of attention

I wish I could take back at least half the times I have said, "You need to pay attention to Momma." I used to think that because my boys were rolling back and forth on the floor while I read aloud, or standing while they completed a math lesson, they were not being attentive (or that someone had slipped them some sugar when I wasn't looking). What I have learned in the past four years of homeschooling is this:

My children are children. Hyperactive or not, movement is a part of how they interact with the world – **including learning**.

For math drills, we jump on the trampoline.

For oral quizzes on books or short stories, we take a walk.

For any and all worksheets, we typically complete them on the floor instead of at the table.

The more I fight it, the less they learn. The more I encourage it, the more they learn.

I wish I could say that I have got this play/move/learn thing all figured out – for my children's sake and my own! I don't, not even close. But the good news is that I am learning.

Fortunately, so are my boys.

Part Four: The Teacher

"At the end of the day, the most overwhelming key to a child's success is the positive involvement of parents." - Jane D. Hull

"I am often the biggest problem in our homeschool. Not my boys, not my husband, not the curriculum or special needs accommodations. Me." – The Author of this Book

Chapter 14: Learning to Ignore "Grade Level"

"He is reading at a first grade level now," I said to the doctor, holding my breath.

"What?" she said with a mix of surprise and concern. *"He's ten."*

I paused for a moment, and decided to ignore the comment welling up in my throat about how I am pretty sure I know how old he is.

"Well, two years ago, he was at a preschool level, so really, he has made two years' worth of progress in two years," I said, sure she would nod her head and appreciate the progress.

She didn't.

We spent the rest of our time together talking about the many options for dyslexia interventions, and getting him to 'grade level'.

I left feeling so sad for my youngest son, who works so hard, but never feels like it is enough.

I understand why he feels this way.

Learning disabilities are so sneaky.

His doctor is well versed in dyslexia and learning differences. She knows exactly what his IQ testing and learning profile mean. She knows the asynchrony of a child profoundly gifted in some areas, and profoundly delayed in others.

And she still cannot believe, after educational therapy and daily instruction for more than two years, that he is only capable of reading Dr. Seuss's Hop On Pop on his best day.

I understand why she feels this way.

Learning disabilities are so sneaky.

We discussed the school vs. homeschool options for him. I used to think he needed to be in school in order to receive the intervention he needs.

I have since learned better, but the doctor surprised me when she said, "*With his needs, there is no way the school system would be able to adequately help him. You might be able to eventually get the school district to pay for him to go to special private school, but that would take years and I am not convinced it would be a good fit for him either."*

"So you see my dilemma," I thought to myself, but did not say.

Learning disabilities are so sneaky.

I came home to my children, exhausted and feeling the weight of it all.

I walked away from the appointment with good advice about all the things I need to do.

And I am grateful for it.

And I am tired of it.

It feels like we are running some sort of race – with grade level as the finish line.

Grade level means nothing to my children.

My oldest is reading at a college level proficiency, but cannot perform sequential tasks, requiring even the most basic executive function.

My youngest is several grade levels ahead in history and science, but couldn't read the word 'said' yesterday.

I cannot use grade level as the standard.

I know this. And yet I long for it. I want progress to be faster and more linear. I want grade level so much it hurts sometimes.

I want to be able to say to anyone who asks, *"Yes, they are at grade level,"* and never again have the discussion about how to speed up their progress.

I want to avoid the panic that rears its ugly head first thing in the morning and last thing at night. "*Am I doing this right? What else can I do? Am I failing these children?*"

My children are children. They are not math equations. They are not projects with completion dates.

As convenient as it would be for them to achieve grade level expectations, this is just simply not possible sometimes. More importantly, when I think about who they are becoming, what matters most in their lifetime, and how they will be most successful as adults, the less reading levels and math standards even matter.

So today, rather than worrying about all the progress we haven't made, I choose to focus on all that my sons have accomplished.

Rather than worrying about grade levels and deficits, I choose to see the computer that my son built in less than two hours, on his own.

I choose to see the book that my little guy picked up, and the true joy with which he read it, rather than the words on the cover – **Step 1 Ready to Read**.

Today, I will do the best that I can for these children.

That means seeing them for who they are and accepting them, exactly where they are, no matter what their grade level.

Chapter 15: Just Because It Is Difficult, Doesn't Mean You Are Doing It Wrong

He threw the book and stomped off to his room.

"*Don't you understand?*" he yelled, clearly frustrated. "*I have dys-A-lexia!*"

As he slammed the door, I tried to sort through a host of reactions – smiling because of the way he pronounced dyslexia, bitter because he threw the book and we have been trying to help him work on the explosive reactions, sad because reading is so very difficult for him, despair because maybe we will never be able to get this right, and grateful because I know he is at least making progress, whether or not we can both see it right this minute.

He came out of his room a few moments later, sheepishly apologized and climbed up on to my lap.

He rested there for a minute, and as I kissed his head and smelled his hair, I asked him what happened.

The only thing he could say was, "**This is too hard. I can't do it right.**"

Several years ago, his older brother suddenly started reacting aggressively and violent towards everyday life. He would lose it every single day, and literally destroy his room and anything or anyone else in the way. He pulled over bookshelves, punched and kicked holes in the wall, hit me in the face, threw heavy objects at my head. He stopped sleeping, preferring instead to cry and bang his head against the wall for hours and hours.

We were on several waiting lists for an evaluation. But waiting lists don't help when it's 3 AM and you have bite marks on your arms, and your baby is slamming his head over and over again into the wall.

I remember sitting next to him, rubbing his back, trying to help him settle down, praying that it would just stop, and saying to myself, **"This is just too hard. I can't do it right."**

When we finally got the diagnosis, I distinctly remember asking the developmental pediatrician what I was "doing wrong" in caring for him. Her answer was so simple.

*"Just because this is hard, doesn't mean you are doing it wrong. It's going to be difficult. **It is difficult**. There is no way around that. But it doesn't mean you are doing it wrong. Sometimes things are just hard."*

I know my son and I are not alone in feeling this way. So many of us want to know how we can fix it, what we aren't doing, what's the right way.

The truth is, sometimes it is just hard.

Sometimes the difficulty level in this game called life is way beyond any of our abilities.

It doesn't mean we are doing it wrong.

I gathered my frustrated boy up in my arms, carried him back over to the table with the books and the flashcards and the pencils, and

I sat down with him. I asked him to face me, looked him straight in the eyes and said –

Just because this is hard, doesn't mean you are doing it wrong.

But we don't quit.

When something is this important, no matter how difficult, we keep going.

Even when we get frustrated. Even when we are sure we can't take it anymore. Even when we know that we are in way over our heads and have no chance of ever not being faced with this circumstance.

We take the next step.

And then the next.

And then the next.

Chapter 16: The Lies I Believe About Being a "Special Needs" Mom

I leaned over the kitchen counter, my head in my hands, and tried to take a few deep breaths.

The house was a disaster, I hadn't finished a reading lesson with my youngest son in three days, I was still in my PJ's at 11AM and thirteen-year-old was melting down over not being able to buy a crested gecko in the next 10 minutes.

So, you know, it was one of *those* days.

As I stood there, trying to force back the tears, trying to get it together, trying not to lose my you know what and either start yelling or drive away in the car, plain as day I had a loud and clear thought –

"You are totally messing this up."

In a moment of pure, Holy Spirit clarity, I thought back to myself, *"Why do I believe these things about myself and these children? I know they are not absolutely true. I know my husband and my friends would never say these things about my mothering."*

The short answer is, they are lies. *(I have a beautiful friend who, upon hearing me actually vocalize one of these lies, grabbed me by the arms, looked straight into my eyes and said, "That is a lie straight from the pit of hell. It is not true." Gotta love a girl who will care for her friend like that and do it with the sweetest, softest southern accented voice…)*

I have spent the last week trying to identify all the lies I am hearing. I am shocked at how often they creep up. I am amazed at how they affect my decision making, my mood, and my mothering.

I found they are all variations of these five soul sucking thoughts –

1. It is Sooooo Different

This one creeps up more often than I would like the admit. When other mommas try to help and speak into my life, I can be prone to thinking, "*Your kids are so great. You have no idea what this is like. My life as a mom is soooooo different than yours.*"

While that might be true on a practical level sometimes, I think the reality is that *it is a lot less different than it is the same*. I have been amazed at how many moms have commented and said, "*My daughter doesn't have autism, but I can completely identify. I think these things too!*"

When my friends and I talk about our children, most of the time we have the same concerns, the same hopes, and the same expectations of motherhood.

2. Maybe The Doctors Got It Wrong

I am not sure why this one still creeps up so much. One day I want to write about the five stages of grief and getting your child's diagnosis, mostly because the denial phase is kinda crazy.

I still, despite all the evidence to the contrary with both of my sons, I still sometimes think maybe those doctors got it all wrong. Maybe it's not that bad. This inevitably leads to the next lie…

3. It's All My Fault

Somehow I believe that I did this. That I ruined both of my kids and although they look like they have autism and dyslexia, it was really me that messed up somewhere along the way and now they are damaged from it.

I know it makes no sense. I know all the research. I can see the obvious genetics in play. Logically, I know this is crazy.

Yet, I honestly still think and operate as if my poor mothering is what caused all of this.

No wonder I am still in my jammies at 11AM.

4. It's Never Going to Get Better, *or conversely*, If I Work Harder It Will All Get Better

I put the two of these together because I find that I tend to ride the pendulum swing between them way too often.

I can find myself totally depressed and actually, whole-heartedly believing that it is never, ever going to get any better than it is right now. I can look back and see all the progress we have made in the past year. I can look ahead to all of the therapies and programs and learning opportunities we will make the most of, and logically know it will change and improve over time. But there are days where I absolutely believe that progress will not happen.

The evil twin of this lie is the polar opposite – *If I just do _____, it will all get better.*

If I could just figure out the right bedtime schedule, find the right homeschool curriculum, add more exercise to our routine, take away screen time, finally get in to see the specialist, find the softest tagless socks, take him to speech therapy…if I could just do all of these things and more, we could make it better.

This one is so yucky. It implies that something needs to be "fixed" about my children. That they are not fearfully and wonderfully made and therefore need to be changed. I am sad that I believe this one so often.

I realize that working to get them the best options for treatment and support is a good thing. Believing that somehow God's plan is not for our good and it is something that I need to change, is so harmful for us all.

5. I Am Failing

And finally, the mother of all the motherhood lies – I am failing.

I let them watch a movie when I should've been baking with them. I am failing.

I let them stay up way past bedtime, not because they had something special, but because I was exhausted and couldn't bring myself to get up off the couch and start the bedtime routine. I am failing.

I let them have cake for breakfast (*again*). I am failing.

I forgot to schedule their 6-month dentist check-up. I am failing.

I didn't make them go to church on Sunday. I am failing.

All of these lies create chaos and confusion and frustration, both in my heart and in my relationship with my children.

And they are just lies.

So today, I pray I choose truth. I pray I choose to believe what my husband and my sweet southern friend and that nice lady at the farmers' market and the doctor we saw two weeks ago believe about me and my sweet boys. I pray I do not dismiss all of these opinions for twisted versions of our life.

Today, I pray we all have the eyes to see us as we truly are.

Messy

Sometimes Failing

Sometimes Victorious

Beautiful

Loud

Stumbling

Working Hard

Loving Each Other

Sinning Against Each Other

A Family Getting It Wrong

A Family Getting It Right

Completely Dependent on Grace

Grateful

Chapter 17: Sometimes We Just Need to Say A Prayer and Eat Some Chocolate

I stayed up way too late last night with certain child of mine obsessing about king snakes and crested geckos…again.

As he started to tell me all about the law in California that allows Field Herping. *"Wait, what is field herping?"* I asked, rubbing my temples and trying to focus.

"Going into the wild and catching your own reptiles," he said.

The internal sarcasm kicked in as my mind raced. *Clearly something I have been hoping for and dreaming about. Me and my son, traipsing through the wilderness, trying not to get any dirt in his crocs, catching wild snakes. Perfect.*

As I tried to pay attention (*for the love, it was almost 1:30 in the morning...sometimes his brain just will not shut down*), I started to think about all the ways I had blown it throughout the day.

1. I am sitting on the couch way too much these days.

2. I left clothes in the washing machine, overnight, again.

3. I had to wash said clothes, again, clearly being a poor steward of our water (*we are in a drought after all*) and of our money (*the water bill went up $14.00 last month – I wonder why. More sarcasm*).

4. I did not have the energy to force him to take a shower last night and I am sure he smells.

5. I could not keep it together when his little brother couldn't recognize the lowercase letter "i" and referred to it as "*you know, this one*" in our reading lesson.

6. I am way behind where I was this time last year in homeschool planning and prep, and now we might get behind.

7. My poor husband hasn't seen me in anything other than raggedy jammies and some helpful but ugly face cream for the last 4 nights. Not that he would ever complain, but still, not sexy.

So, at 1:30 in the morning, I can really take myself out.

I woke up 4 short hours later, depressed and feeling already defeated. I fell back to sleep on the couch and then woke up 20 minutes later, upset that I didn't get in my quiet time to pray and read the Bible (*clearly #8 to add to the list above*).

I am a mess.

And, apparently, I am human.

I am not able to keep it all together and do all the things all the ways I think they should be done.

Special education at home is not for the faint of heart.

It is by far the most challenging thing I have ever done (and likely ever will).

And, it also the most worthwhile.

Even if you ignore every other word I have written in this book, please hear me say this-

We MUST Learn to Give Ourselves Grace.

So, rather than continuing to beat myself up, and to encourage you to give up the same, I have decided to try to speak to myself the way I would one of my friends. I have decided to try and encourage myself and all of you, as I would any of the parents I know and see working so hard for their kids.

I have decided to embrace and extend grace to us.

Dear You and Me,

Of course you are tired and sitting on the couch too much and feeling defeated. You have had an average of 4 hours of nonconsecutive sleep each night for more than a week now. Sleep deprivation is real and you should not beat yourself up because you are not able to accomplish as much. Of course you can't. Here is some chocolate.

Dear You and Me,

At least you did that laundry in the first place. You are working to take care of your family. It matters. If you wash it twice, so what. If you leave it in the basket on the dining room table for three days, it's fine. Your kids are not going to remember and no one is calling CPS anytime soon. Here is some chocolate.

Dear You and Me,

Most 13 year old boys do not enjoy taking a shower. His resistance is partially because of all of his sensory issues and partially because he is completely normal. So are you. Yes, he smells. But he is going to swim tomorrow. That will do. Here is some chocolate.

Dear You and Me,

Yes, it was frustrating when he couldn't for the life of him recall the letter "i". But you know what? Just 6 months ago, he didn't know what it was at all, along with several other letters. And, he read the first two chapters of that book out loud to you this week. Dyslexia is just weird like that. He is making progress. Here is some chocolate.

Dear You and Me,

One of the reasons you homeschool is because it gives you the flexibility to adjust the schedule according to your family's needs. Sleep is your top family priority right now. You know you will figure out the plan. You have for three years running. You will get to it when you get to it. Here's some chocolate.

Dear You and Me,

I know you wish you could keep all this together, but you can't. And you know it. Only Jesus can. He loves you and he loves your family. He's got this. So go take a bath, say a prayer, and eat some chocolate.

With so much love and understanding,

You and Me

About The Author

Shawna is a wife, mother, speaker, and writer. She shares her life as a momma of two special needs children with honesty and humor at www.nottheformerthings.com.

Her writing has been featured at Simple Homeschool, Today.com, The Huffington Post, The Mighty, and Autism Speaks.

She believes that some of the most powerful words in the English language for a parent are, "Me too."

Please feel free to contact Shawna directly at nottheformerthings@gmail.com.

Mail inquiries can be sent to her attention at -

PO Box 11085

Burbank, CA 91510

Made in the USA
San Bernardino, CA
06 February 2017